PRO WRESTLING LEGENDS

Steve Austin
The Story of the Wrestler They Call "Stone Cold"

Ric Flair
The Story of the Wrestler They Call "The Nature Boy"

Bill Goldberg

Bret Hart
The Story of the Wrestler They Call "The Hitman"

The Story of the Wrestler They Call "Hollywood" Hulk Hogan

Kevin Nash

Dallas Page
The Story of the Wrestler They Call "Diamond" Dallas Page

Pro Wrestling's Greatest Tag Teams

Pro Wrestling's Greatest Wars

Pro Wrestling's Most Punishing Finishing Moves

The Story of the Wrestler They Call "The Rock"

Randy Savage
The Story of the Wrestler They Call "Macho Man"

The Story of the Wrestler They Call "Sting"

The Story of the Wrestler They Call "The Undertaker"

Jesse Ventura
The Story of the Wrestler They Call "The Body"

The Women of Pro Wrestling

CHELSEA HOUSE PUBLISHERS

The Women of Pro Wrestling

Kyle Alexander

Chelsea House Publishers
Philadelphia

Produced by Choptank Syndicate, Inc.

Editor and Picture Researcher: Mary Hull
Design and Production: Lisa Hochstein

CHELSEA HOUSE PUBLISHERS

Editor in Chief: Stephen Reginald
Production Manager: Pamela Loos
Art Director: Sara Davis
Director of Photography: Judy L. Hasday
Managing Editor: James D. Gallagher
Senior Production Editor: J. Christopher Higgins
Project Editor: Anne Hill
Cover Illustrator: Keith Trego

Cover Photos: Jeff Eisenberg Sports Photography

The Chelsea House World Wide Web site
address is http://www.chelseahouse.com

First Printing

1 3 5 7 9 8 6 4 2

Library of Congress Cataloging-in-Publication Data

Alexander, Kyle
        Women of pro wrestling / by Kyle Alexander
             p. cm.— (Pro wrestling legends)
        Includes bibliographical references and index.
        Summary: Presents profiles of some of the women who have achieved success
    and fame as wrestlers, managers, and valets in the world of professional wrestling.
        ISBN 0-7910-5839-5 — ISBN 0-7910-5840-9 (pbk.)
        1. Women Wrestlers—Biography—Juvenile literature. [1. Wrestling—Biography.
    2. Women—Biography.] I. Title. II. Series.

GV1196.A1 A44 2000
796.812'082— dc21

                                                                      00-020731

Contents

WOMEN RULE IN A MAN'S WORLD

After 12 years as a professional wrestler, Randy "Macho Man" Savage was, for all intents and purposes, an unknown entity in the sport. He had never won a major title. He had never wrestled in what were, at the time, the three most important federations in professional wrestling: the World Wrestling Federation (WWF), the National Wrestling Alliance (NWA), and the American Wrestling Association (AWA). Floundering around the independent federations, he was a career minor leaguer, a talented man who might have amounted to something if he had only gotten a few breaks. Then he got two. In 1985, the WWF signed him to his first big contract. And at that same time, his wife, Elizabeth, agreed to become his manager.

"A beautiful woman complements me," Savage answered the critics who thought he'd choose a famous man as his manager. "She's a reflection of me, so it's right for her to be my manager."

Within a year, the Macho Man was the proud holder of the Intercontinental title, the second most important singles championship in the World Wrestling Federation (WWF). Elizabeth was second runner-up for *Pro Wrestling Illustrated*'s Manager of the Year honor, marking the first time in the 15-year

---

Chyna, whose real name is Joanie Laurer, made wrestling history on October 17, 1999, when she defeated Jeff Jarrett to become the first woman ever to hold the WWF Intercontinental title.

history of the award that a woman had finished anywhere in the top four.

Elizabeth was the beauty to the Savage beast, the woman who had a calming influence on the man inside and outside the ring. At times she was a distraction, such as when an offbeat wrestler with a green tongue named George "the Animal" Steele fell in love with her. But within a few years, she was not only the most famous woman in wrestling, she was one of the most famous personalities in all of wrestling. Fans weren't always sure whether they loved Savage, but they were head over heels in love with Elizabeth.

A decade later, in 1996, another beautiful woman captured the hearts of wrestling fans everywhere. Her real name was Rena Mero, her ring name was Sable, and hearts skipped a beat when she walked to the ring wearing her skimpy outfits. Hearts broke, too, when it turned out that she was devoted to one of the meanest men in wrestling, Marc Mero.

Mero couldn't accept that the fans were more interested in Sable than they were in him. She was smart, and she could stick up for herself. When Mero and Sable split in 1998, the fans stuck with Sable. His career plummeted while hers soared. She won the WWF women's championship and became one of the most famous personalities in the wrestling world. Her face and figure appeared on the cover of magazines like *TV Guide*, and she pursued a career outside of wrestling.

Then there's Chyna, whose strength and ruthlessness make her the equal of just about any man who steps into the ring. A female bodybuilder, Chyna's huge muscles and imposing

stance are enough to intimidate anybody—male
or female.

On October 17, 1999, Chyna did something
her critics said could not be done. She won the
WWF Intercontinental title, a championship that
had previously been the exclusive province of
men. Using plenty of foreign objects to her
advantage, Chyna defeated veteran grappler
Jeff Jarrett for the belt.

*Sable, who now
goes by her real
name of Rena Mero,
poses with her
husband Marc Mero,
the wrestler formerly
known as Johnny
B. Badd. Both Meros
were signed by the
WWF in 1996, but
in 1999 Rena left
the WWF to pursue
an acting career.*

World champion women's wrestler Mildred Burke strikes a bodybuilding pose. Burke, who was first recognized as the reigning women's champion in 1937, held the title for nearly 20 years.

"Winning the Intercontinental title is a dream come true," Chyna said. "Not only did I win a major title, but I finally put Jeff Jarrett in his place. This victory was good for all the women of the WWF."

Chyna understated her accomplishment. Her victory wasn't merely good for all the women of the WWF, it was a major step forward for women in sports around the world. Imagine a woman winning the world heavyweight championship title in boxing, or starring on an NBA championship team, or hitting two home runs in game seven of the World Series.

From Elizabeth to Sable to Chyna, the women of professional wrestling are a driving force behind the current boom in wrestling popularity.

The history of women in professional wrestling goes back a long way, long before there was a WWF Intercontinental title or a World Championship Wrestling (WCW) telecast. In 1935, Mildred Bliss, a 17-year-old girl from Kansas, tried to talk a promoter into teaching her how to wrestle. Tired of being nagged, the promoter told one of his wrestlers to slam Bliss so hard, she'd stop nagging him. Bliss pinned the man two times. Mildred Bliss changed her name to Mildred Burke and made her living challenging men to wrestling matches.

Women's wrestling had its first boom period in the 1940s, when most young men in the

United States were off fighting in World War II. On October 4, 1949, the woman who would become the most accomplished female wrestler of all time, the Fabulous Moolah, made her debut in Kansas City, Missouri.

The ring has been graced by outstanding female wrestlers such as Moolah, Chyna, June Byers, Mildred Burke, Wendi Richter, Madusa Miceli, and Sherri Martel. It has also benefited from the knowledge and strategies of outstanding female managers such as Elizabeth, Sherri Martel (who went by the name Sensational Sherri), Sunny, and Marlena.

Some women, such as Missy Hyatt, Precious, Baby Doll, Francine, and Dirty White Girl, have served as valets to the male wrestlers. Some women have pushed their men to superstardom, as Elizabeth did with Randy Savage, while others have eclipsed the stardom of the men they were brought in to accompany, as Sable did with Marc Mero.

Women have made the ring a more colorful place. Often, they have made it more beautiful. And sometimes, they have made it a far more violent place. Wrestling is the only professional male sport in which women have played such an important role.

2

MOOLAH . . . AND MORE

The history of women's wrestling in North America began in small theaters at the turn of the century, where women appeared on stage wrestling other women, and sometimes men. Names like Nellie Reville, May Edwards, Texas Mamie, Cora Williams, and Helen Hildreth were standouts of their time, known to the select few people who were aware that women wrestlers even existed.

One of the pioneers of women's wrestling in the United States was Josie Wahlford, a 5' 8", 165-pound powerhouse from New Jersey. She eventually turned to the vaudeville circuit because competition for female wrestlers was so limited in the early 1900s. Another standout of the time was Cora Livingstone of Buffalo, New York, who married a promoter and went on to become recognized as the greatest female wrestler in the world.

But not until the 1930s did women's wrestling move from the carnival sideshows and vaudeville theaters to respectable arenas, where women wrestled on the same cards as men. One woman, in particular, will always be known as the mother of women's wrestling in North America. Her name is Mildred Burke.

June Byers lands a drop kick on world champion Mildred Burke's chest during a December 12, 1949, match in Denver, Colorado. Burke, who managed to retain her title, often joked that wrestling was not as dangerous as housework.

MILDRED BURKE

Born in Coffeyville, Kansas, in 1915, Mildred
Burke, along with Billy Wolfe, the man who
would become her husband, introduced America
to women's professional wrestling. At this time
female wrestlers were considered oddities at
best and freaks at worst. Burke saw her first
pro wrestling match at age 19 and was hooked
immediately.

Wolfe agreed to train Burke, who was a nat-
ural athlete. But there wasn't much competition
for her. Most women wrestled only on vaudeville stages. They were showgirls, not wrestlers.
So Burke decided to wrestle men. Wolfe would
put up $25 for any man or woman who could
pin Burke in 10 minutes, as long as the man
didn't outweigh her by more than 20 pounds.
For two years, she went unbeaten.

The next step for Burke was getting recognized not as a sideshow act, but as an athlete
in legitimate wrestling arenas. Her first arena
match was against a 140-pound man, and the
show sold out in six hours. At first, the man
didn't want to wrestle Burke. He was persuaded
to return, however—and lost to Mildred in eight
minutes.

Because of this amazing performance, Burke
suddenly had no trouble getting work on men's
wrestling cards. She became one of wrestling's
hottest draws, and the cards on which she
appeared usually sold out. Suddenly, more
women were drawn to the ring. Often, they
asked Burke to train them.

In 1937 Burke and Wolfe moved to the
South. The recognized women's world champion
at the time was Clara Mortensen, who out-
weighed the 5' 2", 140-pound Burke by more

than 30 pounds. They wrestled twice, each woman winning once. The final match was held in Chattanooga, Tennessee, and it was one of the roughest women's matches ever wrestled. Burke won and was recognized as the women's champion for most of the next 20 years.

Burke was not only a great wrestler, she was a genuine celebrity. Her fans included the great jazz singer Al Jolson. She appeared in *Ripley's Believe It Or Not* for doing 100 body bridges on a desk. After 21 years and more than 6,000 matches, Burke retired in 1955. She remained involved in the sport, however, until she died in 1989. Her legacy lives on as she claimed to have trained over 2,000 women wrestlers.

Clara Mortensen stands in a dressing room in 1937, when she was the women's wrestling world champion. Mortensen, who hailed from Glendale, California, lost her title to Mildred Burke later that year.

JUNE BYERS

On August 20, 1954, Mildred Burke's incredible unbeaten streak came to a shocking end. She wrestled June Byers in a best-of-three falls match in Atlanta, Georgia, and when the one-hour time limit expired, Byers had scored the only fall. She was named the new women's champion.

Byers, like Burke, wrestled for Billy Wolfe's promotion, and Penny Banner, a great ring star of the 1950s and '60s, described her as "the greatest wrestler I ever faced."

Byers came along just as Burke's career was winding down. Women's wrestling needed a new standard-bearer, and Byers was made for the part. Born DeAlva Snyder in Houston, Texas, she grew up watching Friday-night wrestling on her family's black-and-white TV. Her uncle, lightweight wrestler Ottoway Roberts, worked for a wrestling promoter in Houston. At age seven, little DeAlva was already training for a career in the ring.

She was spotted in Texas years later by Wolfe, who asked her what she thought about becoming a professional wrestler. She told him she had thought about it quite a bit, and before long, she was on a train to Columbus, Ohio, to begin her new career under a new name, June Byers. She made her debut in 1944 in a women's battle royal in Virginia.

For years, Byers got numerous shots at Burke, the women's champion, but was unable to beat her. She did, however, win the tag team title with Millie Stafford. The fans loved her.

"I took every match and every opponent very seriously," Byers said. "Every time I climbed into the ring, it was my goal to make that match the best I could. That may sound silly, that I was always nervous before wrestling, but I always gave each match my best. I always wrestled to win, and I always tried to give the fans the best possible ring action that I was capable of."

Her best was more than good enough. She left Wolfe's promotion and won another women's title in a 13-woman battle royal in Baltimore. After defeating Mildred Burke in 1954, Byers remained the women's champion until her retirement in 1964,

THE FABULOUS MOOLAH

In 1999, the Fabulous Moolah won the WWF World women's title—more than 43 years after she had won the women's world title for the first time. For excellence over a long period of time, no athlete in history can match Moolah.

She was born Lillian Ellison in Columbia, South Carolina. She never revealed her true age. When she first approached promoter Billy Wolfe about becoming a wrestler, he told her, "You're too small to wrestle. Go sit on some lawyer's knee and be a secretary."

June Byers receives the Girls' World Championship Wrestling belt from James Holmes, Chairman of the Maryland State Athletic Commission. In 1954 Byers defeated Mildred Burke to become the new champion of women's wrestling.

But Lillian Ellison had no intention of spending her life as a secretary or sitting on anybody's knee. Lillian followed her heart and became a wrestler. She made her ring debut in 1954 in Massachusetts. Moolah was so impressive in her early matches that she was invited to enter a tournament for the NWA World women's title on September 18, 1956, in Baltimore. She won, beating Judy Grable in the tournament final. She remained an NWA champion for most of the next 28 years.

Moolah didn't suffer her first loss until 10 years after she won the title. On September 17, 1966, she lost to the little-known Betty

Boucher in Seattle, Washington. She regained the title two months later, and held it for another two years before losing to Yukiko Tomoe in Osaka, Japan. Moolah regained the belt a month later and held it for another eight years.

Finally, on July 23, 1984, in Madison Square Garden, Moolah lost the title to Wendi Richter in one of the most famous matches in wrestling history. The match was signed because of an argument between legendary wrestler/manager Captain Lou Albano and music star Cyndi Lauper. Lauper, who managed Richter, challenged Albano, who called upon Moolah to do his dirty work. Moolah and Richter were opposite in every way. Moolah was a rough, rugged brawler who didn't care about appearances. Richter was a rock 'n' wrestling glamour girl. Richter won the match and the title.

Fifteen years later, Richter's ring career was long over, and Moolah, a 10-time women's world champion, was still going strong. In 1995, the Fabulous Moolah was inducted into the WWF Hall of Fame.

PENNY BANNER

Penny Banner was the glamour girl of women's professional wrestling in the 1950s and '60s. Banner was called the "Wow Girl" for a publicity photo that she took wearing a string bikini. In those days, women simply didn't wear string bikinis, especially in publicity photos.

She was dazzling, she was beautiful, and she could wrestle. Her real name was Mary Ann Kostecki. She got her start wrestling for promoter Billy Wolfe, and quickly changed her name to Penny Banner, which was easier to pronounce. That's how Mary Ann Kostecki became Penny

Banner. The new name was much easier to pronounce.

Penny took her first step toward fame when she took a judo class at a YMCA and was noticed by Sam Muchnick, who was then president of the NWA. Impressed, he called in Penny for a tryout. She made the grade.

Penny started winning matches in Ohio, Kentucky, and Tennessee. She challenged June Byers, but Byers was reluctant to wrestle her. Then Penny saw a newspaper ad which said

A leopard-suited Penny Banner, at right, executes a flying toss on Judy Glover, sending her through the air during their 1955 match in Washington, D.C., which Banner won.

that Byers was taking on all challengers. Penny walked up to the ring in Columbus, Ohio, and challenged Byers. She took the world champion to a 10-minute time-limit draw. Months later, Penny beat Byers in two tough matches.

On August 26, 1961, Banner became the first AWA women's champion. She later won the Western Canada tag team title with Betty Hawkins, and the women's world tag team title with Lorraine Johnson. But Penny got married shortly afterwards and had a daughter. Tired of being away from her family, Penny stepped away from the ring. A superb athlete, she has since won medals in the Senior Olympic Games.

MAE YOUNG

Mae Young was a bad girl, maybe the greatest villain in the history of women's professional wrestling, and certainly one of the toughest.

Young wrestled in the 1950s and was never able to win the women's world title from Mildred Burke or June Byers, but she had some incredibly tough and violent matches with both champions. Her feud with Mae Weston is considered the most intense in women's wrestling history.

Young had attitude, and was among the very first wrestlers to strut into the ring—an idea that was later copied by Buddy Rogers and Ric Flair. After retiring, she trained many top women wrestlers, and even in her sixties, she occasionally teamed up with the Fabulous Moolah.

VIVIAN VACHON

Vivian Vachon was born into wrestling. Her brothers, Maurice "Mad Dog" Vachon and Paul

"Butcher" Vachon, would go on to become professional wrestlers. Maybe that's why people said Vivian Vachon wrestled like a man.

There was nothing polite about her. Vachon was a power wrestler, just like her brothers. She was big at 155 pounds, and she never gave mercy to an opponent, whether she was slamming them inside the ring, or kicking them in the stomach outside the ring. She was fast and had incredible endurance.

Vachon had other talents, too. She made some hit records (in French) in Quebec, Canada. She was also the subject of the movie, *Wrestling Queen*. Vivian Vachon died in 1991 in a head-on automobile collision. She was 40. Her legend lives on through her niece, Luna Vachon.

3

HERE COME THE VALETS

By the 1980s, anybody who paid attention to professional wrestling knew that women could wrestle, yet interest in women's wrestling was waning. The major federations—the WWF, the NWA, and the AWA—began scheduling fewer and fewer women's matches, and before long it was rare to have a women's match on more than one card a month.

That didn't mean there were fewer women who wanted to make their living in professional wrestling, it simply meant that they'd have to start using their beauty and their brains, instead of just their brawn.

In the mid-1980s, pro wrestling was enjoying a boom in popularity, and women were there to help it along. Wrestling fans tuned in each week to watch Hulk Hogan and Ric Flair stake their places among the all-time greats, but they also tuned in to sneak a peek at some of the beauties of the ring.

These were the days of women like Elizabeth, Missy Hyatt, Precious, Baby Doll, and Woman. There was Sunshine, who had some amazing battles with both Missy Hyatt and Precious. Jeannie Clark sided with a young Steve Austin in his feud with Chris Adams and his wife, Toni Adams. Later, Toni turned against her husband, starting another feud. There was Dirty White Girl, the femme fatale to "Dirty White Boy" Tony

---

After being fired from WCW, where she was coannouncer with Jim Ross, Missy Hyatt began working as a wrestling commentator for the AWF. Hyatt has also been a valet for wrestlers like the Sandman and Shane Douglas.

Anthony. Baby Doll both aided and feuded with the legendary Dusty Rhodes. Dark Journey got into some horrific catfights with Missy Hyatt.

These women didn't merely accompany their men to the ring—they aided and abetted, interfered, and became a part of the personality of professional wrestling, adding significant color to a growing sport.

ELIZABETH

In 1985, when Randy "Macho Man" Savage arrived in the WWF and went looking for a manager, everybody assumed he'd pick one of the famous big names who were courting his services, men such as Mr. Fuji, Bobby Heenan, Fred Blassie, Johnny Valiant, and Jimmy Hart. Savage never considered any one of them. He only had eyes for one person—his wife, Elizabeth. At the time few people knew Elizabeth was his wife, but they certainly knew this: she was one of the most beautiful women to enter the ring in a long, long time.

She was sweet, almost Cinderella-like in appearance with her pretty face, brown hair, and petite figure. A world of male wrestling fans fell in love with her. And the more Savage mistreated her, the more fans wondered, "Why does she put up with him?"

Elizabeth wasn't merely the beautiful woman who accompanied Savage to the ring and softened his image. She was his manager, directing his career. Savage had never won a major title until he called Elizabeth to his side. She was both a brilliant business manager and an inspirational presence, convincing Savage to go after the WWF Intercontinental title then held by Tito Santana. When Savage beat

Santana for the belt, much of the credit belonged to her.

Elizabeth's fame soured with a chapter of her career that can only be called, "Beauty and the Beast." George "the Animal" Steele developed a crush on Elizabeth and started bringing her flowers. Elizabeth enjoyed the attention, but Savage was enraged. When Steele picked up Elizabeth and carried her backstage, an enraged Savage chased after Steele and beat him up.

Elizabeth was always too much of a distraction for Savage. His jealousy ended his partnership with Hulk Hogan, merely because he thought Hogan had his eye on Elizabeth. Savage and Elizabeth eventually had a public wedding at SummerSlam '91, but the marriage didn't last long.

Elizabeth, at center, turned Randy "Macho Man" Savage's career around when she became his manager in 1985. Elizabeth was one of the most successful female valets in wrestling and helped Savage, left, win titles in both the WWF and WCW.

The soap opera of Savage and Elizabeth carried through the 1990s. As the new millennium began, Elizabeth was no longer the darling of the wrestling world. She had become hated as a result of her association with the rulebreaking Hogan-led New World Order (NWO) in WCW.

MISSY HYATT

A blonde, and sometimes a redhead, with a voice that has both annoyed and fascinated listeners, Missy Hyatt became the pinup girl for professional wrestling at a time when most people thought of the Fabulous Moolah when they thought of women in the ring.

Missy Hyatt looked and acted nothing like the Fabulous Moolah. She was a conniver who whined and always made certain she got her way.

The 5' 8", 129-pound blonde bombshell made her wrestling debut in 1985 in Texas, when she was the valet for "Hollywood" John Tatum in World Class Championship Wrestling. Tatum, who fashioned himself as a glamour boy, was the perfect match for Missy, who considered herself a glamour queen.

But Missy didn't make a name for herself until a year later, when Tatum moved to the Universal Wrestling Federation (UWF). She loved working in the UWF. "It was all still new to me and exciting and fun," she said.

In addition to working together in the ring, Tatum and Missy were a couple. But then Missy caught the eye of "Hot Stuff" Eddie Gilbert. Before long, Gilbert's outside-the-ring courting of Missy turned into a vicious inside-the-ring feud with Tatum. The entire wrestling world watched with fascination each week on the UWF's television shows as Missy slowly danced her way into Gilbert's arms.

Missy's fame magnified after the UWF disbanded, and she got her first big-time job working as a television commentator and valet in WCW. Missy was fired by WCW in 1994, and worked as a commentator in the American Wrestling Federation (AWF), as a valet for Sandman and Shane Douglas in Extreme Championship Wrestling (ECW), and also in the United States Wrestling Alliance (USWA) and National Championship Wrestling (NCW). She could later be seen wrestling for independent federations throughout the northeastern United States.

WOMAN

In the late 1980s, wrestling fans were fascinated by a strikingly gorgeous, petite woman who had lush brown hair and wore unusual outfits, including leather miniskirts, spiked gloves that went halfway up her arms, and makeup that made her look like a Halloween nightmare. Her name was Fallen Angel, and she was the valet for one of the most corrupt and offbeat wrestlers the sport has ever seen, Kevin Sullivan.

Fallen Angel underwent several identity changes. When she signed with WCW, she changed her name to Robin Green and nearly led Rick Steiner down the road to ruin after he fell in love with her. She switched her name to Woman when she started managing the tag team Doom.

By no means did Woman take a subservient role in the ring. Far from being an innocent bystander, she was downright evil and interfered whenever she had the opportunity.

*Woman, who was
known for her
ruthlessness and
cunning, worked
with wrestlers
like Kevin Sullivan,
Doom, and the Sand-
man, and was one
of the most popular
managers in pro
wrestling.*

Eventually, she became a respectable manager, and finished fourth in votes for *Pro Wrestling Illustrated*'s Manager of the Year in 1995.

Woman left WCW and signed with ECW, where she managed Sandman before returning to WCW. Classier and more refined, she changed to cocktail dresses and started wearing her hair straight and even added a bow.

"There isn't anyone who has followed the sport for more than a day that doesn't know of my abilities, my history, my influence, and my strategic knowledge," she told *The Wrestler* magazine. "I know the art of psychological warfare as well as anyone alive, and I use it, and I am proud to flaunt it. Because I have nothing to fear. Those who have something to fear are those who stray too close to my web of power and influence."

PRECIOUS

There were actually two valets named Precious in the 1980s: Precious I and Precious II. Both were blonde and beautiful. Neither could be trusted. And both were the valets for "Gorgeous" Jim Garvin, who liked nothing better than looking at himself in the mirror and having beautiful women on his arms.

Actually, there was one thing he liked almost as much: winning any way he could. Both women named Precious were always eager to help.

Precious I lasted a bit longer than Precious II, and she was best known for spraying Garvin's opponents in the eyes with a caustic mist. Precious was at her best during Jim Garvin's 1988 feud with Ric Flair, which had Flair complaining, "The Garvins are driving me crazy!" Actually, it was Precious who was driving him crazy.

Precious was unusual because back in the 1980s, wrestling fans weren't used to despising the women who made their living in the ring. They somehow expected women to have a softer touch and to add some class to the sport. But Precious was nasty and never sweet.

4

THEY CAN WRESTLE, TOO

I n the mid-1980s, a woman's place in professional wrestling was uncertain at best. There were the beautiful valets, such as Missy Hyatt and Dark Journey, who captured the attention of wrestling fans, but what about a woman who wanted to be an athlete and compete in the ring? These women had to work hard. First, a potential female wrestler had to fight to get noticed. Then she had to fight to get matches. Finally, and most difficult of all, she had to fight to get wrestling fans to notice and care.

The 1980s were a hot time for pro wrestling, but women like Wendi Richter and Madusa Micelli had to work harder than the women before them to get respect in the ring. That they succeeded against the odds is an everlasting testament to their greatness.

WENDI RICHTER

The year was 1984 and professional wrestling was a fringe sport. True, there were some cities in which it was nearly impossible to get a ticket to the monthly wrestling card, but in 1984 the world had never heard of pay-per-view television, WCW's *Nitro*, or WWF's *Raw*, and most people had never heard of a wrestler named Hulk Hogan.

One of the most violent women wrestlers in the WWF, Luna Vachon is the niece of wrestling legends Vivian, Paul, and Maurice Vachon.

When pro wrestling moved to the forefront of American entertainment in 1984, a woman was leading the move. Her name was Wendi Richter, "the Texas Cowgirl."

Richter's rise to fame occurred in a round-about way. The 5' 7", 140-pound native of Dallas, Texas, had been wrestling for several years when, in 1984, manager Captain Lou Albano got into an argument with pop music star Cyndi Lauper. When Lauper challenged Albano, he called upon the women's world champion the Fabulous Moolah to fight for him, while Lauper called upon Richter. The rock 'n' wrestling connection was born.

Richter vs. Moolah, with Lauper and Albano in their respective corners, was one of the most hyped matches in wrestling history. The match, held on July 23, 1984, at Madison

Known as "the Texas Cowgirl," Wendi Richter rose to fame in 1984, when, under the management of rock star Cyndi Lauper, she defeated the Fabulous Moolah at Madison Square Garden to become the new champion of women's wrestling.

Square Garden, was billed as "The Brawl to Settle It All" and it was aired on MTV. With millions of wrestling fans tuning in, as well as millions of people who had never before watched a wrestling match, Richter defeated Moolah, thereby ending Moolah's 28-year domination of women's wrestling.

Richter and Hulk Hogan became the main players in the WWF's rock 'n' wrestling connection, which changed the sport and increased its popularity immeasurably. In 1986, Richter was featured on the cover of *Pro Wrestling Illustrated* under the headline, "Women's Wrestling Comes of Age: Is Wendi Richter More Popular than Hulk Hogan?"

Hogan turned out to be the most popular wrestler in history, while Richter's fame was fleeting. But she made the most of her short stay in the spotlight.

Richter lost the title to Leilani Kai on February 18, 1985, but regained it in a highly touted match at WrestleMania I. Finally, the Fabulous Moolah summoned up a big effort and defeated Richter for the title on November 25, 1985. After the loss, Richter left the WWF.

Richter continued her wresting career in Puerto Rico, won the World Wrestling Council women's title, and wrestled for the NWA and the National Wrestling Federation (NWF), but she never regained the glory of that one brief period when she was the hottest wrestler, male or female, in the entire sport. The mark she made on the sport will never be forgotten.

SHERRI MARTEL

Known as Scary Sherri, Sister Sherri, and Sensational Sherri, Martel managed such

Sherri Martel, who was trained by the Fabulous Moolah, won three AWA women's titles before becoming a successful manager for wrestlers like Randy Savage, Shawn Michaels, Ric Flair, and Harlem Heat.

wrestling standouts as Shawn Michaels, Randy Savage, Ted DiBiase, Buddy Rose, Doug Somers, Harlem Heat, Shane Douglas, and Ric Flair, while holding her own in the ring.

Sherri Martel, whose real name is Sherry Russell, began her wrestling career in the 1980s. She was trained by the Fabulous Moolah and brought a fierce killer instinct to her matches. The 5' 7", 130-pound Martel looked elegant in the ring, but she was as fierce as a tiger. She won her first of three AWA World women's titles in 1985 by beating Candi Devine. Martel proved she could be doubly successful, too, by managing AWA World tag team champions Buddy Rose and Doug Somers.

Martel got her big break in 1987 when she jumped to the WWF and defeated the Fabulous Moolah for the WWF World women's title. Just when her wrestling career was hitting its stride, Martel decided to trade in her tights for more business-like outfits. She focused on managing full-time and made her first major mark by signing Randy "Macho Man" Savage in the late 1980s. Savage's feud with Hulk Hogan, and Sherri's feud with Elizabeth, was one of the top-drawing cards of 1989.

She managed Savage and Shawn Michaels in the WWF, and Ric Flair and world tag team champions Harlem Heat in WCW. Wherever she has gone, and whatever she has done, Sherri Martel has always been the center of attention.

MADUSA MICELLI

As recently as 1999, she was a member of Randy Savage's beautiful entourage, but Madusa Micelli didn't always use her striking good looks to get attention in the ring. Back in the late 1980s and early 1990s, Madusa Micelli staked her claim as one of the greatest female wrestlers of all time. She is one of three women, along with Wendi Richter and Sherri Martel, who have held world women's titles in two separate federations.

Born Debra Ann Micelli in Milan, Italy, the 5' 9", 150-pound Micelli studied to be a nurse and did some modeling before beginning her wrestling career in 1985. It wasn't until 1987 that she made wrestling her full-time profession. She wrestled in the now-defunct AWA and had a rocky start, losing to Sherri Martel at SuperClash II on May 2, 1987. But it didn't take long for Madusa to get her ring career into full gear. On December 27, 1987, she defeated the heavily favored Candi Devine to capture the vacant AWA World women's title. She held the belt for nearly a year before losing to Wendi Richter on November 26, 1988.

Like many other female wrestlers of this era, Micelli turned to managing and, for a time, she guided the careers of Curt Hennig and Eddie Gilbert. But wrestling was her first love, and after leaving the AWA she signed with All-Japan Women's Wrestling. On January 4, 1989, Madusa defeated Chigusa Nagayo for the International Wrestling Association (IWA) World women's title. She held the belt for only a day, but regained it the following September.

Madusa was a standout in Japan, where women's wrestling is nearly as popular as men's wrestling. Her combination of power, skill, and endurance fascinated the fans. She spent three years in Japan and Thailand, where she also honed her kickboxing skills.

After leaving Japan, Madusa signed with WCW, where she managed Rick Rude. She also made headlines in some unusual ways—she wrestled male manager Paul E. Dangerously to a draw, and she lost a bikini contest to Missy Hyatt. But in WCW, it seemed as if Madusa's looks and managerial ability were more important than her wrestling ability, so in 1993 she signed with the WWF and took on the name Alundra Blayze.

On December 23, 1993, Madusa defeated Heidi Lee Morgan for the vacant WWF World

Madusa Micelli, bottom, struggles to break out of Luna Vachon's chokehold. Micelli, who has held world women's titles in the AWA, IWA, and WWF, has often said that U.S. fans do not respect women wrestlers.

women's title. She held the belt until November 20, 1994, when she lost it to archrival Bull Nakano. Madusa had heated feuds with both Nakano and Bertha Faye, and won the belt three times before leaving the federation in 1995.

Madusa departed from the WWF in dramatic style; she appeared on WCW's *Nitro* and threw the WWF women's title belt into a garbage can.

In WCW, Madusa was unable to wrest the women's title from Akira Hokuto, who forced her into retirement with a victory at the 1997 Great American Bash.

Despite all of her success and popularity, Madusa's career was marked by frustration over her inability to make women's wrestling more popular. She wished fans in the United States respected female wrestlers as much as Japanese fans did, but she suspected that might never happen, so she was forced to take a backseat to male wrestlers in the U.S.

BULL NAKANO

What's it liked to be loved by millions of fans around the world? Don't ask Bull Nakano; she couldn't tell you. Nakano got more than her share of respect and fear, but no love. Along with Devil Masami, she was the woman Japanese fans loved to hate. In fact, she was the woman wrestling fans all over the world despised. Nakano held the All-Japan World Women's Wrestling Association (WWWA) tag team title several times, the All-Japan World women's title, and the Empressa Mundial de Lucha Libre (EMLL) women's title in Mexico. But the belt she was most proud of was the WWF World women's title she took from Alundra Blayze on November 20, 1994. Nakano held the title for five months before losing it back to Blayze.

She had some huge wins over the great Akira Hokuto in Las Vegas and in 1987, Chigusa Nagayo for the All-Japan women's title. She shared the All-Japan women's tag team title with Dump Matsumoto, Candor Saito, and Kumoko Iwamoto.

Offbeat, vicious, and anything but polite, Bull Nakano brought ultra-violence to women's professional wrestling. "I may not be seen as the most beautiful woman in the world, although I am very beautiful in my own way," Nakano once told *The Wrestler* magazine. "There are many men who can attest to that. But I am undeniably viewed as the most feared woman in the world. And that is something of which I am very, very proud."

LUNA VACHON

She's vicious and she's a woman to be feared. She comes from the same family that produced Paul "Butcher" Vachon, Maurice "Mad Dog" Vachon, and brawling female wrestler Vivian Vachon. Born into a legacy of violence, Luna Vachon carried the legacy forward with pride.

When Luna appeared in frightening face makeup, spiked leather outfits, and an ever-present scowl, wrestling fans had no problem picking the side of her opponent. They went against her when Luna had a wild feud with Sable. The fans went for the beauty and in this battle, Luna was clearly the beast.

While hanging around with WWF wrestlers such as the Godfather and battling for the WWF World women's title, Luna was more concerned with destroying her opponents than just winning matches.

A STRUGGLE
FOR IDENTITY

5

As wrestling underwent significant changes in the early and mid-1990s, so too did women's roles in the sport. Television exposure multiplied, thanks to Monday night programs like WCW's *Nitro* and WWF's *Raw*. Glamour and glitz took on a more significant role in the sport. Male wrestlers, desperate for attention, brought in beautiful women as their sidekicks. More often than not, these women got involved in the action.

Beulah McGillicutty went from magazine centerfold to wrestling goddess. Francine Fournier became the "Head Cheerleader" of ECW. Marlena had fans wondering, "Who—or, rather, what—is that woman?" Lori Fullington staked her claim to fame in the mid-1990s when she and her three children turned against her husband, the Sandman, in ECW. "I am trying to rein in the violence in Extreme Championship Wrestling," Fullington explained. "Everyone in the sport, unfortunately, wants more, more, more. Somebody's gotta stand up and say, 'Enough!'"

Much to her consternation, nobody listened. In some ways, her situation was a microcosm of what was happening to women's wrestling as a whole: a lot was happening, but not many people were paying attention.

As wrestling's television ratings increased, women wrestlers got more exposure than ever before. One of the WWF's rising female stars is Tori, left, shown fending off an attack from Ivory, the two-time women's champion.

41

BEULAH MCGILLICUTTY

There have been women in wrestling who first became noticed for their brains, women who first became noticed for their athletic ability, and women who first became noticed for their beauty. Beulah McGillicutty, a former model, belonged in the final category. A legion of admiring fans gave Beulah a claim to fame in the 1990s.

"I don't think I am the most important woman in the sport, I know I am the most important woman in the sport," she said at the peak of her fame in 1997. Confidence was not a problem for Beulah.

Born Theresa Hayes in Philadelphia, Pennsylvania, Beulah entered ECW in a most unusual way. Raven had a surprise for his rival, Tommy Dreamer: "the fat girl from summer camp that nobody liked" was coming to ECW in 1995 to help him out. The fat girl from summer camp, no longer fat and now quite beautiful, was Beulah.

Later that night, she helped Raven beat Dreamer by spraying hairspray in Dreamer's eyes. From then on, it seemed as if every time Dreamer wrestled Raven, he would be the victim of some dastardly scheme by Beulah.

The fans couldn't get enough of her, but Dreamer had too much of her. At Hostile City Showdown '95, Dreamer was beating Raven when Stevie Richards, Raven's partner, tried to interfere. Beulah interfered, and Dreamer piledrived her.

Beulah's relationship with Raven ended when Raven attacked her and Dreamer came to her rescue. ECW fans watched in disbelief as Dreamer and Beulah embraced. Later, Dreamer would have two valets: Beulah and Kimona, making him, in some eyes, the luckiest man in wrestling. Beulah later became known for her off-again, on-again friendship and feud with Francine.

FRANCINE

Born Francine Fournier on February 19, 1972, Tommy Dreamer's "Head Cheerleader" might not be the most beautiful woman in wrestling history, but she's certainly one of the most outrageous.

Introduced to the sport in 1995 through ECW, a federation that prides itself on hardcore violence, Francine, a former insurance agent, liked to tell her fans and enemies, "I'm going to show you how hardcore I can be."

Francine has gotten herself involved in numerous brawls, not only with the other women of ECW, but with ECW's male wrestlers. In 1999 she teamed with Tommy Dreamer to win several tag team matches against Steve Corino and Dawn Marie. That feud started when Corino rudely interrupted Dreamer's retirement speech, and Corino further paid for his bad behavior when Francine wrestled him in several mixed one-on-one matches, beating him most of the time. Often, she used her version of the "Stone Cold stunner" made famous by WWF star Steve Austin. She also had a long-running feud with Tammy Lynn Sytch, also known as Sunny.

ECW fans first became aware of Francine in 1995 when she sat in the stands and cheered her hero, Stevie Richards. Her regular appearances at ECW cards began to wear on the nerves of Richards's mentor, Raven, and his valet, Beulah McGillicutty. That led to a legendary showdown between Beulah and Francine, in which both women tore into each other with a fury seldom seen by men or women in the ring. But Richards turned against Francine by surprising her with a kick, enabling Beulah to score the pin.

Francine, the Queen of Extreme, went on to manage the Pit Bulls, Shane Douglas, and, finally, Dreamer. In October 1995, she led the Pit Bulls to the ECW tag team title. In 1996, she helped Pit Bull II and Shane Douglas win the ECW TV title. She claimed her first ECW heavyweight title when Douglas beat Sabu on August 17, 1997, and led Douglas to another ECW heavyweight championship in 1999. She has also led the teams of Chris Candido and Lance Storm and Dreamer and Raven to the ECW tag belts.

Francine's goal was to leave her mark on professional wrestling as the most influential woman ever. "The sport is changing, and it's changing quickly, and it's changing in my favor," she said. "I don't have to bend over backward to accommodate the sport, the sport is going to accommodate me. If you want to judge me by my beauty alone, fine, that's exactly what I want. Because while everybody is focused on my body, my mind is working, plotting, planning for the day when this is all mine."

TERRI RUNNELS

The woman WWF fans now know as Terri Runnels has had a lot of different identities. Her real name was Terri Boatwright, but she began her pro wrestling managing career in 1990

Sunny, also known as Tammy Lynn Sytch, had a long feud with Francine. Francine wanted to be the most influential woman in pro wrestling, but it was Sunny who was voted Manager of the Year by the readers of Pro Wrestling Illustrated *in 1996.*

as Alexandra York, the bespectacled business suit-wearing, computer-carrying accountant of Michael Wall Street, previously known as Mike Rotundo. When Rotundo left WCW, York started the York Foundation—comprised of Terry Taylor, Rick Morton, and Tommy Rich—and they benefited from York's intelligence. She turned Terry into Terrance, Rick into Richard, and Tommy into Thomas. She made them better men and better wrestlers.

In 1991, York was second runner-up for *Pro Wrestling Illustrated*'s Manager of the Year for her part in leading Terrance, Richard, and Thomas to the WCW six-man tag team title. She was the female valet turned business manager, a woman for the 1990s in a sport that too often was light years behind in its treatment of women.

Her next identity was unveiled several years later. In 1995, Dustin Runnels—her husband—jumped from WCW to the WWF and became Goldust, a bizarre character who dressed from head to toe in gold and wore a blond wig. At the 1996 Royal Rumble, Razor Ramon defended his Intercontinental title against Goldust, who

Marlena was offbeat, but she couldn't hold a candle to her husband, Goldust, who was one of the strangest characters in the WWF.

came to the ring with a mysterious blonde beauty. She wore a gold cocktail dress. During the match, she sat in a director's chair smoking a cigar. Her name was Marlena, formerly known as Alexandra York.

Marlena played an important role in the match. Several times, Goldust hid behind her. Finally, she stepped onto the ring apron, faked a sprained ankle, and fell onto the referee. The 1-2-3 Kid—now known as X-Pac—stormed the ring and floored Ramon, allowing Goldust to score the pin and win his first Intercontinental title.

If Goldust was the most bizarre wrestler in the WWF, then Marlena was the most bizarre woman the sport had ever seen. Goldust was such an offbeat character that, by extension, any woman who hung out with him had to be outrageous. She constantly interfered in Goldust's matches, and one time inadvertently caused him to be stripped of the I-C title. But she helped him get it back by distracting the referee, enabling Goldust to pin Savio Vega for his second Intercontinental championship.

Marlena often found herself embroiled in controversy. Hunter Hearst Helmsley tried to steal her away from Goldust, but when Triple-H brought in Chyna as his bodyguard, Marlena was equal to the task, surviving every one of Chyna's brutal attacks.

Goldust lost the title to Ahmed Johnson and was unable to regain the belt from Helmsley, who beat him in a classic matchup at WrestleMania XIII. A few weeks later, Marlena was at Goldust's side on *Monday Night Raw* when Goldust removed his face paint and, in a poignant interview, revealed that Marlena was his wife, Terri.

Marlena left wrestling for about a year, went home, took care of her daughter, and returned in 1999 as Terri Runnels, Val Venis's femme fatale. Several attempted reunions with Goldust didn't work out, and her relationship with Venis ended. She and Jacqueline teamed up to step through the ropes and take on Venis and Marc Mero. Ryan Shamrock joined Terri and Jacqueline, forming the trio known as Pretty Mean Sisters.

Terri then went on to manage the Hardy Boys, Matt and Jeff Hardy, to the WWF World tag team title.

MADD MAXINE

If she had to get by on her beauty, Madd Maxine would never have stood a chance in professional wrestling. But Madd Maxine never had to rely on her looks to get what she wanted. She relied on her ability.

She sported wild hair. Her face makeup—heavy on the black around the eyes, heavy on the white on the rest of her unusual visage—was downright frightening. She had a killer instinct unmatched by any female wrestler in the world and many male wrestlers, too.

More than 60 years after Mildred Burke took on male opponents as a gimmick to make money, Madd Maxine wrestled males in the Pro Wrestling Federation (PWF) for one reason: she wanted to win the PWF heavyweight title.

In 1995 Madd Maxine was not only one of the best female wrestlers in the world, but according to Pro Wrestling Illustrated's annual "PWI 500" ranking, she was the 315th best wrestler in the world, male or female. She beat nearly every top male wrestler in the PWF, including Austin Steele, Tyrone Knox, Flaming Youth, and Masked Maniac. She became one of the first women to win what had previously been considered a men's championship when she won the PWF junior heavyweight title in 1996.

Unfortunately for Madd Maxine, she began to pile up so many victories that men stopped wanting to wrestle her, fearing that they would be embarrassed. She managed several wrestlers for a while, including the Russian Assassin, then retired from the ring.

6 THE NEW BREED

As the 1990s drew to a close and a new millennium began, several major personalities emerged to redefine women's roles in what had been a predominantly men's sport. Women can be whatever they want to be in wrestling, and roles that were previously reserved strictly for men or women are now open to all participants

SABLE

She was born in Jacksonville, Florida, on August 8, 1967, the second oldest of four kids. Her name was Rena. Nearly 30 years later, she became Sable, the most recognized personality in professional wrestling. In a sport ruled by big, strong, violent men, this beautiful blonde captured the hearts and imagination of millions of men and women around the world.

Before introducing herself to wrestling, she modeled for Guess? jeans, Pepsi, L'Oreal, and Bongo, and also shot a video for MTV. One night, Rena was out to dinner with her friends when she got a note from a man sitting at another table.

"The note said, 'Do you like me? Yes or no. Circle one,'" she recalls. "I waited about 20 minutes and sent the note back with a circle and in that circle I wrote, 'Maybe' and a smile from me. To my surprise, he came over to our table and

During an evening gown match in 1999, Debra McMichael defeated Sable for the WWF World women's title.

braved the gauntlet of my girlfriends to talk to me. His name was Marc Mero."

After a year, they started to go out, and eventually married. When Mero signed with the WWF in 1995, the WWF decided to sign his wife, too. That's how Rena Mero became Sable.

Sable first appeared at WrestleMania XII on March 31, 1996, accompanying Hunter Hearst Helmsley to the ring. When he lost the match, Triple-H blamed Sable, and Mero came to her rescue. The next night at *Monday Night Raw*, Sable left the building in Mero's arms.

Mero, however wanted the spotlight to shine only on himself, even if there was a beautiful woman at his side. Mero won the Intercontinental title later in 1996, but he couldn't deal with the idea that the fans were more interested in Sable than they were in him.

Sable, however, was not willing to be subservient to a man. She got more aggressive. She won two awards—Dressed to Kill and Miss Slammy—at the 1997 Slammy Awards. She also had in-ring arguments with Mero. The tension between Mero and Sable was put on hold for a while as Sable feuded with Luna Vachon, but it couldn't be ignored. Shortly after Sable used Mero's finishing move, the TKO, to beat Vachon at WrestleMania XIV, Mero and Sable had their in-ring split. On May 31, 1998, Mero beat Sable in a loser-leaves-the-federation match.

Sable proved time and again that she was more than a pretty face. On November 15, 1998, she used her "Sable bomb" finisher to defeat Jacquelyn for the WWF World women's title. She later feuded with Debra, but lost the title to her under dubious circumstances.

Meanwhile, Sable had become a national phenomenon. She appeared on the cover of *TV Guide* magazine, and was a guest on *The Tonight Show with Jay Leno*.

Then, in 1999, Sable's relationship with the WWF came to a crashing conclusion when she filed a $110-million lawsuit against the federation, alleging improper working conditions. The lawsuit was settled out of court and prohibited her from using the name Sable. She is now Rena Mero.

"Six years of wrestling, three years of modeling, I was due for a change," she said. "Got to keep moving and reaching for the stars! I now hope to have the opportunity to pursue my true ambition, acting. I love being in front of the camera."

DEBRA

In the mid-1980s, Debra was the "Queen of WCW," a conceited former pageant queen who had represented both Texas and Illinois in various beauty pageants, but who had no credentials to be a wrestling manager. Then, in 1985, while Debra was on a flight to Chicago, she met the mother of Chicago Bears football player Steve McMichael, who convinced her to go out with her son. Sparks flew, and they eventually married.

In 1995 Steve McMichael started announcing on WCW's *Monday Nitro*. When Ric Flair made some negative comments about Debra, McMichael recruited Kevin Greene to join him in a tag team match against Arn Anderson and Flair. McMichael turned against Greene during the match and joined the Four Horsemen.

Sable used her "Sable bomb" finisher on Jacquelyn to win the WWF women's championship in 1998. But less than a year later, unhappy with the way she was treated in the WWF, Sable filed a lawsuit against the federation, alleging improper working conditions.

Debra didn't have much of a role in the sport, other than to decorate Steve's arm when he walked to the ring. She wanted the opportunity to show what she could do, so she created her own opportunity.

In 1997 Debra turned against her husband and joined up with Jeff Jarrett. The feud pitting the Horsemen against Jarrett, Eddy Guerrero, and Debra was one of the hottest of the year, and culminated with McMichael beating Jarrett for the U.S. title at Clash of the Champions XXXV on August 21, 1997.

Debra began the next stage of her career in October 1998, when she signed with the WWF and began managing Jarrett. Wearing short business suits instead of short dresses, she used her deadly charm to distract Jarrett's opponents. On January 25, 1999, Jarrett and Owen Hart won the WWF World tag team championship.

Debra also won the WWF World women's title on May 10, 1999, when she beat Sable in an evening gown match. Toward the end of 1999, Debra ended her relationship with Jarrett by smashing him over the head with a guitar.

CHYNA

The first woman to win the WWF Intercontinental title, Chyna has been bodyguard, manager, and wrestler during her brief but spectacular career. If Sable and Debra repre-

In 1998 Debra managed her client, Jeff Jarrett, left, to a WWF World tag team title with Owen Hart.

sent the softer side of women in wrestling, then Chyna represents the tougher side. She has a muscular physique most men would envy.

Born Joanie Laurer in Rochester, New York, on December 27, 1970, Chyna didn't have it easy growing up. Her father was an alcoholic and her mother was married five times. She moved out of her house when she was 15 years old, eventually attended the University of Tampa, and took on a wide array of jobs such as selling beepers, singing in bands, and working as a bartender, airline attendant, and belly dancer.

When she was young, she hated wrestling. But she loved staying in shape, so when she was 16, she started lifting weights. Seeing her muscles respond thrilled her, and weightlifting became more than a hobby—it became an obsession. After graduating from college in 1992, she joined the Peace Corps. When her tour of duty ended, she returned to the United States and worked at odd jobs until fate led her to Killer Kowalski's wrestling school in Massachusetts.

She was a quick study, thanks to her athletic ability and her already-hardened physique. She wrestled on the independent circuit and found it to be a hard life. She also competed in the Fitness America Pageant and tried her hand at women's boxing. Then, in February 1997, WWF wrestler Hunter Hearst Helmsley, who was looking for a bodyguard, called her. She accepted his offer. Soon afterward, Joanie Laurer became Chyna.

Helmsley and Chyna combined with Shawn Michaels to create the clique known as D-Generation X. She constantly interfered in

Helmsley's matches against Rocky Maivia, and so enraged Maivia that he challenged her to a match.

Chyna proved herself not only as a bodyguard, but as a wrestler, too. She was the first woman to compete in both the Royal Rumble and the King of the Ring tournament. At the No Mercy pay-per-view in October 1999, she beat Jeff Jarrett for the Intercontinental title.

KIMBERLY

Kimberly, who hails from Chicago, attended Auburn University and North-western University and has degrees in public relations, journalism, and marketing. Before becoming one of the hottest stars in professional wrestling—and the founder and leader of WCW's famous Nitro Girls—Kimberly worked in public relations as a junior account executive.

In 1989 she met wrestler/manager "Diamond" Dallas Page, and the two were married in 1991. Later that year, Page started bringing Kimberly to the ring as one of his "Diamond Dolls," a bevy of beautiful women. Eventually, he brought only Kimberly with him to the ring.

Page, however, didn't treat Kimberly very nicely. His ego doomed their partnership, and he eventually lost Kimberly's services to Johnny B. Badd, and then the Booty Man. In 1997, however, Kimberly and DDP teamed up once again. It happened after Kimberly and Page posed for a magazine. Randy Savage and Elizabeth got hold of the magazine and taunted Page and Kimberly, igniting a feud that was

Since signing with the WWF, Chyna has become the first woman to compete in events like the Royal Rumble and King of the Ring. She was also the first woman to win the WWF Intercontinental title.

voted Feud of the Year in 1997 by the readers
of *Pro Wrestling Illustrated* magazine.

Page stopped bringing Kimberly to the ring
for his matches, but that didn't stop Kimberly
from making her mark in another way. She
founded the WCW Nitro Girls dance team.

"I knew we were going to be successful, but
the team has exceeded even my expectations,"
Kimberly said. "We work as a team. Each of the
girls bring different talents and backgrounds to
the table. The sum is greater than the parts."

Kimberly, however, remains the behind-the-
scenes manager for her husband. "I still do all
the managerial work that I did before," she
says. "I just don't stay at ringside. When Page
has a match, I am always standing behind the
curtain watching the match."

As for her performances with the Nitro
Girls, Kimberly says: "I just go out there and
have a good time and forget everything but
what we're about: fun!"

SUNNY

The woman now known as Tammy Lynn Sytch
in ECW didn't have it easy when she tried to get
her start in professional wrestling in the early
1990s.

She made her debut in Smoky Mountain
Wrestling (SMW) in 1993 as Brian Lee's manag-
er. She led Lee to the SMW heavyweight cham-
pionship, and also feuded with Dirty White Girl.
In 1994, when Lee lost the SMW title, she
brought Chris Candido into her stable. Lee and
Candido teamed to win the SMW tag team title.
When they later lost the belts, Tammy fired Lee.

In 1995 Candido signed with the WWF and
entered the federation without a manager.

Tammy worked for the WWF as an announcer and commentator, using the name Tamara Murphy. After a few weeks, she resumed her duties as Candido's manager. He was Skip, she was Sunny. When Candido went into a slump, Sytch teamed him with Tom Prichard, who became known as Zip.

Skip and Zip were known as the Bodydonnas, and Sunny's interference helped them win the WWF World tag team title in 1996, but their good times didn't last long. The Godwinns won the belts from the Bodydonnas, and Sunny jumped ship, joining the new tag team champions. Then she jumped ship again, joining the Smokin' Gunns when they won the belts. "I just follow the money trail," Sunny said.

Following the money trail helped Sunny become one of the best managers in the sport. In 1996, she was voted Manager of the Year by the readers of *Pro Wrestling Illustrated* magazine. In 1998, she was a runner-up for Manager of the Year after leaving the WWF and signing with ECW. As 1999 drew to a close, she was managing Candido under the name Tammy Lynn Sytch and undoubtedly plotting her campaigns for 2000 and beyond.

Today's fabulous women of wrestling combine brains and beauty with tremendous wrestling skill. Often, they don't care whether their opponent is a woman or a man. Nearly a century ago, the great Mildred Burke introduced America to women's wrestling. If she came back today, she might not recognize what she created . . . but she would probably love every bit of it!

Chronology

1937   Mildred Burke wins the world women's title from Clara Mortensen

1954   June Byers beats Burke for the world women's title on August 20

1956   The Fabulous Moolah wins the world women's title by defeating Judy Grable in a tournament final on September 18

1984   Moolah loses the WWF World women's title to Wendi Richter at "The Brawl to Settle It All" at Madison Square Garden on July 23

1985   Lelani Kai wins the WWF World women's championship from Richter at Madison Square Garden on February 18; Richter regains the WWF World women's title from Kai at WrestleMania II; Moolah, wrestling as Spider Lady, wins the WWF World women's title from Richter on November 25

1987   Sherri Martel wins the WWF World women's title from the Fabulous Moolah

1993   Alundra Blayze—Madusa Micelli—beats Heidi Lee Morgan in a tournament final for the vacant WWF World women's title on December 23

1994   Bull Nakano beats Blayze for the WWF World women's title in Tokyo, Japan on November 20

1995   Blazye regains the WWF World women's title from Nakano; Bertha Faye beats Blayze for the WWF World women's title; Blayze defeats Faye for the WWF World women's title on October 23, 1995, moves to WCW, and dumps the belt in the trash

1998   Jacquelyn beats Sable in a tournament final for the vacant WWF World women's belt; Sable wins the WWF World women's title from Jacquelyn on November 15

1999   Debra McMichael wins the WWF World women's title from Sable on May 10; Chyna defeats Jeff Jarrett to become the first woman to win the WWF Intercontinental title

Further Reading

Albano, Lou, et al. *The Complete Idiot's Guide to Pro Wrestling.* New York: Macmillan, 1999.

Burkett, Harry. "Elizabeth's Warning to Gorgeous George: You've Unleashed the Madness—Watch Out!" *The Wrestler* (October 1999): 38–41.

"Chyna Breaks Down the Wall." *WOW Magazine* (December 1999): 36–44.

Ethier, Bryan. "The Women of the WWF: There's More to Their Power than Their Looks." *Pro Wrestling Illustrated* (November 1999): 24–27.

Hunter, Matt. *Superstars of Men's Pro Wrestling.* Philadelphia: Chelsea House Publishers, 1998.

Mazer, Sharon. *Professional Wrestling: Sport and Spectacle.* Jackson: University Press of Mississippi, 1998.

"Meet the Women—Up Close and Personal." *Pro Wrestling Illustrated Presents* (Vol. 1, No. 1): 68–93.

"She'll Only Keep Her Sunny Side Up." The Wrestler *Presents True Life Stories* (Summer 1998): 28–42.

"The Top 50 Women Wrestlers of All-Time." *Pro Wrestling Illustrated Presents* (Vol. 1, No. 1): 6–33.

"Traveling the World in Search of Chyna." The Wrestler *Presents True Life Stories* (Summer 1998): 48–57.

Index

KYLE ALEXANDER has been involved in the publication of professional wrestling magazines for more than a decade. His previously published volumes about professional wrestling include *The Story of The Wrestler They Call "Sting"* and *Bill Goldberg*. Over the past 10 years, he has made numerous appearances on radio and television, offering his unique perspective on the "sport of kings."